# Chasing The Dawn

Verses of Resilience, Unveiling Her Story

Krritika Singh

BookLeaf Publishing

India | USA | UK

Made with ❤ on the BookLeaf Publishing Platform
www.bookleafpub.in
www.bookleafpub.com

# Dedication

This book is dedicated to my family, with special love and gratitude to my grandmother, Maya. She was the bedrock of my life—the source of my strength, confidence, and everything I strive to be. Though she is no longer with us, her presence remains in my heart, growing stronger with each passing day. Grandma, I miss you a little more every day.

# Preface

This collection of poems is a heartfelt exploration of resilience, transformation, and the indomitable spirit of womanhood. Divided into three sections, it weaves together the journeys of two women while paying homage to all who have faced life's trials with strength and grace.

The first section (poems 1–10) paints a vivid portrait of my sister-in-law's life. Though she had a joyful childhood, her world was shaken by the loss of her parents at a very early age. These poems capture her strength as she navigated the challenges of growing up without them, finding her way through life with remarkable determination and grace. It is a celebration of the incredible woman she has become—a source of inspiration for everyone around her.

The second section (poems 11–18) delves into my own life—a narrative shaped by the weight of societal stigma. These poems reflect on my childhood, the mental scars it left, and the journey through my teens and twenties, where I was molded into someone I didn't fully recognize. Now, in my thirties, as I look back, I see the fragments of my true self emerging, yearning to be whole again. This section is an honest reflection of the battles within and the courage to heal.

The final section (poems 19–21) is a tribute—a celebration of young girls and women who embody resilience and hope. It honors their untold stories, their quiet strength, and their boundless potential to rise above challenges.
This book is more than poetry; it is a testament to life's complexities and triumphs, an ode to the strength of women, and a reminder that through reflection and connection, we all find pieces of ourselves.

With gratitude and love,
Krritika Singh

# Acknowledgements

With a heart full of gratitude, I extend my deepest thanks to the extraordinary people in my life who have been my guiding light, inspiration, and unwavering support on this creative journey.

To my grandfather and father, I owe the gift of creativity —the spark that ignites my love for writing. Your wisdom, stories, and passion for expression have shaped my imagination and given me the courage to put my thoughts into words.

To my mother, you are my moral compass, my greatest teacher in the art of humanity. Your unwavering love and belief in me inspire me to strive to be a better person every single day.

To my husband, my rock and my partner in every dream, thank you for standing beside me in everything I want to achieve. Your encouragement fuels my confidence and keeps me moving forward.

To my sister-in-law, thank you for being the muse behind so many of these poems. Your courage and resilience have touched my heart deeply, compelling me to pen down my admiration for you.

To my daughter, the moment you entered my life, everything changed for the better. You are my light, my joy, and my greatest transformation. Being your parent is my most cherished role.

To my family - Papa, Mum, Bua, Swati, Rishi, Vishakha, Apurva, Rajat, Shiv Raj, Rajesh, Amandeep, Swara, Atira, Raghav, and Amita - you are my strength, my foundation, and my reason to smile. Your love and support surround me like a shield, and I am endlessly grateful for each of you. I love you all more than words can ever convey.

This book is a reflection of all the love, inspiration, and strength you have poured into my life. Thank you for being my world.

With all my love,
Krritika Singh

# 1. A Star is Born

With restless heart and mind full of prayer,
he paced the floor, lost in hope and care.

Waiting outside the room, an endless endeavour,
overwhelming thoughts made him glare.

Inside, she was calm, so uniquely prepared,
a family of three now to be declared.

She closed her eyes, emotions surged,
love and warmth washed over every inch, once scared.

Walking haphazardly, anxiety crept in-
*"Is my wife alright?"* was all he'd think.

Excited to embrace motherhood, she was ready to bring,
a sudden cry rang out in a blink.

The pacing stopped, the worry eased,
with the cry, his joy was released.

Bliss filled the air,
she asked the doctor, *"Am I blessed with a boy or a girl
as our heir?"*

*"The heavens must weep for sending this gem to earth.
Ma'am, you're blessed with a beautiful girl."*

He walked into the room as his wife cuddled their
daughter,
*"Congratulations, Mr. Kalia, your princess is here."*

*"As bright as the sun, our shining star,
she'll reign in her realm—our princess is born to go far."*

# 2. The Joy of Parenthood

With boundless love and care,
they welcomed their heir.
Life overflowing with joy,
happiness filled the air.

The house became a home,
alive with laughter.
For now, they have a daughter,
to cherish ever after.

Friends and family gathered,
to greet their little angel.
With smiles, they said,
*"It's a girl! And soon, a brother she'll bring—so special!"*

Parents beamed and said,
*"Our girl holds immense potential.
One day, she'll rise to fame,
with a name truly substantial."*

*"The journey of parenthood,
a gift from our firstborn.
Our daughter, our beginning,
forever to be adorned."*

*"So, dear ones, welcome our little girl
with all your heart.
Gift her the best childhood,
as her life is set to start."*

# 3. A Symphony of Childhood

Little girl's life is now filled with love,
Her world a reflection of heaven above.

Mama's care and Papa's affection,
She found everything in life that caught her attention.

Her father, the source of her confidence,
She became her mother's precedence.

Her parents, her shield from every distress,
She grew up like a true princess.

Her childhood is now a symphony of euphoria,
A melody that lingers, like sweet, eternal gloria.

# 4. Woven in Bonds

As the girl grew, she found a company,
A brother joined her life, now part of her journey.

She loved her brother as much as her mother,
Calling him her support, like no other.

Everything in her life was like the sweet springtime,
Days filled with the warmth of a cordial chime, so
sublime.

The presence of relatives always brought contentment,
Her home was a place of endless entertainment.

The cousins, a perfect blend of chaos and calm,
Her world bathed in the magic of charm.

It felt as if God had waved his magic wand,
Surrounded by a family, united in a never-ending bond.

# 5. When Life Shifts, Family Remains

Childhood faded, and adolescence began,
Everything that was fun now has a plan.

Relatives parted, it wasn't like before,
They were left alone, a family of four.

Happiness and joy prevailed just like earlier,
With loving mama, caring papa, and adorable brother—
what more could be dearer?

While the little girl is now in her teen,
Sometimes she felt life was being mean.

Something that once brought contentment,
Their differences replaced it with disappointment.

She missed her childhood every day a little,
She never knew relationships could be this fragile.

By now, she understood that people change and can be
distant,
But deep in her heart, she knew her family would be her
constant.

# 6. From Carefree to Concerned

The responsibilities replaced carefree in a hurry,
Adulthood brought in anxiety and worry.

Life was transforming with every moment,
It was becoming the next action plan proponent.

Everything that once brought happiness
Was slowly disappearing into the darkness.

Parents' health was now compromised,
Gradually, life felt like a tragedy disguised.

Her source of confidence was diminishing,
Papa's health was just worsening.

Once her mama's precedence,
Now she longs for her soothing presence.

Parents departed, never to be back again,
And at such a young age, the home that was once like
heaven, felt more like an orphanage.

The little girl had changed, life turned her into a woman,
Carrying a baggage of questions, left alone.

# 7. Born to Shine, Reborn in Strength

Within four months, she lost her parents, her constants,
A hopeless life brought along a heartbreak-resistant stance.

Her story of a happily ever after changed for no good reason,
And home felt nothing less than a prison.

Her mind flooded with overwhelming thoughts,
The family that once gave her strength, now no longer sought.

With her brother, she cried her eyes out,
Mustered all her courage to once again stand tall.

She reminded herself she was born to shine,
Wiped the tears rolling down her cheeks and decided to be fine.

As easy as it seemed, it could never be,
After all, it was just herself and her little brother, and no one to see.

With every passing day, the stress found its way,
She had now become a home of anxieties, as everyone
would say.

With her constant gone, she reminded herself why she
was born,
Just like her mother said, *"She'll reign in her realm, our
star is reborn."*

# 8. The Bond Beyond

Rising from the storm was not something she could do
alone,
Her brother beside her was the only one who was her
own.

Days passed by without others' support,
Only a few friends stood by as her only resort.

Within a few months, she found another home,
Leaving her brother behind was a thought she'd never
known.

Assured by her brother, *"I will thrive by myself; your life
must flourish,"*
With a promise of being inseparable, she found her
prince charming to cherish.

A new life and a new family brought a smile to her face,
Yet the baggage of emotions she left behind refused to
erase.

Each day, she felt something was missing in her life,
The worry of her brother living alone cut through her
like a knife.

Her brother was someone who yearned to be her
strength,
He worked hard to ensure his sister soared at length.

With every step he took, he paved her way,
A bond unbroken, come what may.

The princess, as she was called, must reign in her realm,
Now on her way to steer the helm.

With dreams ablaze and her vision engraved,
She builds the empire she always craved.

# 9. Seeking Love, Embracing Hope

Children without parents, they were called,
The void left by her parents could never become small.

Longing for her father's strength and her mother's
warmth,
She began seeking love, like a mother, in every person's
heart.

Years passed by, and she has now made peace with the
inevitable,
With her husband by her side and her brother with her,
she is now stable.

Everything is now settling as per plan,
Her brother shifting to a different city was something
she never thought she'd withstand.

With a heavy heart and eyes full of tears,
She said, *"You don't know how much I will miss you,
dear."*

Life goes on, she thought with grace,
Motherhood is something that she is ready to embrace.

*"Oh, dear life, why can't you bestow love like you did?*
*Just one child is all I need."*

So many years in marriage have passed on,
She was praying for a baby, just one.

Weeping silently, she wipes her tear,
*"Come what may, I am ready to steer clear."*

*"The show must go on, I must fight,*
*Come what may, I will make it right."*

# 10. Reign of the Resilient

While the country celebrates the arrival of Lord Ram in
Ayodhya,
She welcomed her beautiful son after fourteen years in
euphoria.

For a mother, she craved for all those years,
Motherhood was something that could only cheer.

With gratitude in her heart and appreciation deep
within,
She thanked the universe for everything it was bringing.

Life was filled with joy after so long,
Her son brought back the happiness that had been long
gone.

She now has plans for everything she once desired,
After all, she is born to reign in her empire.

The journey of the little girl to a woman was not very
easy,
Transforming from a princess to a queen was never
breezy.

With everything so good around,
Life brought something to astound.

It brought darkness every time she tried to stand alone,
But remember, she is a star who will keep chasing the
dawn.

# 11. Written on God's Slate

A cherished talk, the granddaughter home after a long while,
She returned to her favourite room, her grandparents'—
so divine.

*"Heaven must be weeping as I reached Earth for my new beginning."*
The girl teased her granny, *"Maya, tell me, what was it like when I was here, grinning?"*

Maya recited her birth story, *"Sweety, you are right, heaven was howling.*
*The day had thunderstorms roaring, rain pouring, and wind whistling.'"*

*"Interesting!"* said the granddaughter. *"Tell me more about me.*
*Darling, you were smiling with wide-open eyes, full of glee."*

*"Is it true? Did I exactly look like this when I appeared?*
*True! Everyone said, "Little one, you're wise beyond your years."*

*"Dear Maa, then why did they say, "Sad, it's again a girl"?
Did they not welcome my arrival as I entered this
world?"*

*"Is it that bad to have two daughters? Please tell me
more.
No, it is not. We were on cloud nine; you were our core."*

*"Then why didn't society celebrate the second daughter?
Darling, everyone is born with their own fortune; how
does it matter?"*

*"You brought your own fate, and we were there to
celebrate.
We love you dearly, you are our everything; everything
is written on God's slate."*

# 12. Shadows of Judgment

Now is the time for a trip down memory lane,
After twenty long years, she boarded the train again.
Childhood was beautiful, but those shadows brought pain,
They carried baggage that forever would remain.

The memories flashed, taking her childhood away,
She recalled them like nightmares haunting the day.
She remembered how they could not let her childhood stay,
For everyone lies, saying childhood is all happiness and play.

*"Dear God, what did I do wrong to be blessed with this skin?*
*Everyone says I'm not beautiful, neither my relatives nor kin.*
*How can I wash away this color to be prettier, to be seen?*
*It's all a lie when they say that beauty lies within."*

The school haunts, no longer feels like a safe place,
Where classmates did all they could to bring disgrace.
*"How does it matter to society, the color of my face?*

*Fair or dark, how can I win in this race?"*

*"The guy who sits next to me calls me black, fat, buffalo,*
*Why is it that everyone's thoughts are so shallow?*
*At home, they say, "Wear brighter clothes, it will be*
*more mellow,"*
*How do I tell them, every day, shadeism is the poison I*
*swallow?"*

*"Oh! You cannot get her married, she is so dark,"*
The relatives discuss this at home and make such
remarks.
*"Is this how the world will evaluate me and leave its*
*mark?*
*How do I get rid of this color? The thoughts inside me*
*just barked."*

The tear rolled down her cheek after so many years,
*"Dear society, you made me an attention seeker, unable*
*to do anything but shed tears.*
*You can call them Achilles' heels, laugh at them, and*
*cheer,*
*But thank you for your concerns—this, I must say,*
*changed my life in every sphere."*

# 13. Echoes of a Shattered Childhood

The memories trickled down from her eyes, slowly,
This wasn't the only thing that made her feel so lowly.
She recalled her past, each moment vividly,
The shadow of that one soul brought vengeful fear so
gravelly.

Relatives made harsh remarks, but one among them hurt
her soul,
He did things that stole her childhood, leaving her
happiness untold.
His presence caused a never-healing wound, a heart with
a hole,
While he lingered, her soul withered, unable to speak,
scared of society's toll.

She has now started fearing his presence,
This one haunts her more, leaving her ashamed in
essence.
*"Oh, how do I fight him?"* It dawns on her sense,
That society's rejection would be so immense.

*"Do I have a choice to defeat him and stand tall?*
*He cannot make me feel so small each day, after all.*

*I must muster courage; it's not the time to fall,*
*Oh, don't you know? I'm not a rebel without a cause."*

*"The repeated incidents are making me so sad,*
*This suppressed anger turns revengefully bad.*
*Now I want to be heard, seen amidst the crowd,*
*Thank you for stealing my childhood; you must be*
*proud."*

# 14. Shields of the Past

By now, she was sobbing uncontrollably,
Her bitter childhood memories had left her soul charred
deeply.

She built a boundary, a shield to keep the world barred,
A desperate resort to protect herself, to stay on guard.

As tears streamed down, plunging her further into
sorrow,
She reflected on a life that felt like it was borrowed.

A life judged at every step, scrutinized so thorough,
Where her yesterday relentlessly shaped her tomorrow.

Everything she endured in childhood shaped who she is
today,
She wasn't herself deep inside but chose to live a
different way.

It felt like an invisible war where she had to slay,
A constant battle to prove her worth every single day.

People labelled her stubborn, egoistic, and hard to
befriend,

But to her, friendship, relationship, and society were
myths in the end.

Armed with a superiority complex to prove she's the
perfect fit,
She transformed into a relentless contender, never ready
to quit.

# 15. From My Childhood to Yours

Back to reality, where she now stands in her thirties,
She asks Maya, *"Don't you think my childhood shaped this modality?"*
*"The personality I carried through my teens was born of causality,*
*Little did I know, I could have at least focused on my true personality."*

*"My childhood shaped my future, made me rigid,*
*All the actions I took then remain so vivid.*
*I wish someone had embraced me, like magic divine,*
*Perhaps I'd have become a better version of mine."*

Maya said, *"Darling, you still have a long way to go,*
*All that you endured then, I'm truly sorry to know.*
*Everything you were, and all you've become, I take a bow,*
*You are my precious granddaughter, my pride, whom God has bestowed."*

*"Maa, one thing I will make sure,"*
*The soul that is growing inside me, so pure,*
*I will protect her all my life and keep her secure.*

*She will have a wonderful childhood, that I will ensure."*

Maya spoke, *"I am waiting for my great-grandchild,*
*She will be everything like you, oh so kind,*
*I am overjoyed, absolutely on cloud nine.*
*The child will be a mini-you, whom you can call mine."*

# 16. The Essence of Motherhood

She asked Maya, *"Maa, tell me, what would motherhood*
*be like?*
*Will it be about how we survive?*
*Will it be about the way we strive?*
*Will it be about our sacrifice?*
*Will it be about the compromises?"*

Maya replied with a sigh,
*"It's about the soul inside,*
*It's about the first cry,*
*It's about when she arrives,*
*It's about the lullabies,*
*It's about when you seek, and she hides.*
*It's about when she confides,*
*It's about being a source of life,*
*That's how earth becomes paradise,*
*That's how the world survives,*
*That's when mankind revives.*
*It's about that another life."*

# 17. Generations of Love

A few months down the line,
She held her in her arms and called her mine.

She looked at Maya and said,
*"Maa, I've made myself home to be called her loving mom.*
*My heart skipped a beat when I heard her heartbeat,*
*My breath was taken away when she took her first breath, I must say.*
*There were tears in my eyes when I heard her cry,*
*Her smile is the reason that can make me walk an extra mile.*
*All the words seem few; I must admit, my life is renewed,*
*My world belongs to her, it's all so new."*

*"The lessons of motherhood you gave have made me strong and brave,*
*Maa why don't you say anything now?*
*You told me you wanted to meet her—it was your vow.*
*I wish you could hold her, share your warmth,*
*Instead, you decided to take an early depart.*
*The motherhood journey felt so known,*
*Without you, I feel all alone."*

# 18. Love at First Sight

She caressed her daughter, holding her tight,
*"Oh, is this what they call love at first sight?*
*Honey, you've made my world so bright,*
*Motherhood, in its truest sense, is pure delight."*

*"Until now, I never realised,*
*How someone could mean more than my life.*
*Everything changed for the better the moment you*
*arrived,*
*You're a bundle of joy, reviving my childhood, so alive."*

*"The journey of motherhood feels so unique,*
*I've known you for lifetimes, now I truly think.*
*There's a deep connection between us I can feel,*
*A blessing from above, my forever, oh so sweet."*

*"I vow to protect you every day of my life,*
*I'll be your guardian for as long as I survive.*
*You're my inspiration, the reason I thrive,*
*Dear daughter, I wish for your happiness to forever*
*arrive."*

# 19. The Journey of Tiny Feet

Tiny feet were set to fleet,
To meet the world and to greet.
Like a blank canvas, she let them imprint.

Subsistence first, she must pay heed,
Cognizance next is what she will need.
Discretion third, upon which society feeds,
Swank is last, but not the least.

Tiny feet were set to fleet,
And found this world incomplete.
She dreamed of a world so sweet,
Where she could chase her dreams with feat.

But the world came with its decree,
And weighed her down with its decree.
Tiny feet were set to fleet,
Yet they longed for a world replete.

# 20. Walked Alone, Smiled Strong

I have walked miles alone,
Rejoicing in my victory,
Distressed at defeat, yet I've shone.

One step at a time—my life's song.
Every milestone achieved,
Gave me lifelong memories to cling on.

*"Let go of your fear,"* my soul said decidedly,
I choose happiness over every anxiety.
The story of my life will be recited mightily,
I have walked miles with a smile, I proclaim proudly.

# 21. A Tribute to Women

She is a beautiful soul,
Mother, daughter, sister, wife—she has many roles.
She works her charm in every relationship so whole,
She is a puzzle that is unsolved.

She is someone who effortlessly blends,
A person easy to befriend.
She is everything for a family, from beginning to end,
She is a summary difficult to comprehend.

She consists of an essence of nature,
A mother who nurtures.
She thinks through the future,
She is a person not easy to be allured.

She is bold and modest,
A human who possesses too much strength, the
strongest.
She is tender and toughest,
She is everything who cannot be understood even the
slightest.

She is a one-man army,
People around her are always happy.

She can be calm as a breeze and yet stormy,
She is God's creation, the feminine.
She is a woman—a beautiful soul.